Housatonic River Fly Fishing Guide

Bill Guebenin in Two Car Hole when the sun "gets off the water," the evening dry-fly fishing can start early.

Picturesque northwest Connecticut is home to many seeking refuge from the pressure of the big cities. The area has many working farms.

JOHN BELLOWS

Typical Housy brown.

HOUSATONIC RIVER
Fly Fishing Guide

JEFF PASSANTE

About the Author

Jeff Passante is a Connecticut native with over forty years of fly-fishing experience and is a past president of the Housatonic Fly Fishermen's Association. He has fished the Housatonic for over twenty years. A retired telephone company manager, Jeff has written articles for *Fly Fisherman* and *Fly Tyer* magazines.

©1998 by Jeff Passante

All rights reserved. No part of this book may be reproduced without the written consent of the publisher, except in the case of brief excerpts in critical reviews and articles.

All inquiries should be addressed to:
Frank Amato Publications, Inc.
P.O. Box 82112 • Portland, Oregon 97282 • 503-653-8108

Book Design: Amy Tomlinson
Cover photos:
Top: John Bellows   Bottom: Jeff Passante
Fly photos by Jim Schollmeyer
All other photos by Jeff Passante unless otherwise noted.

ISBN: 1-57188-151-4   UPC: 0-66066-00349-2

Printed in Canada
1 3 5 7 9 10 8 6 4 2

Table of Contents

Introduction   7

Chapter One: **Equipment**   9

Chapter Two: **Dam Releases**   12

Chapter Three: **The Hatches and How to Fish Them**   17

Chapter Four: **Fishing Non-Hatch Periods**   32

Chapter Five: **Smallmouth Bass Fishing**   34

Fly Patterns

Trout Flies   42

Bass Flies   54

The Housatonic

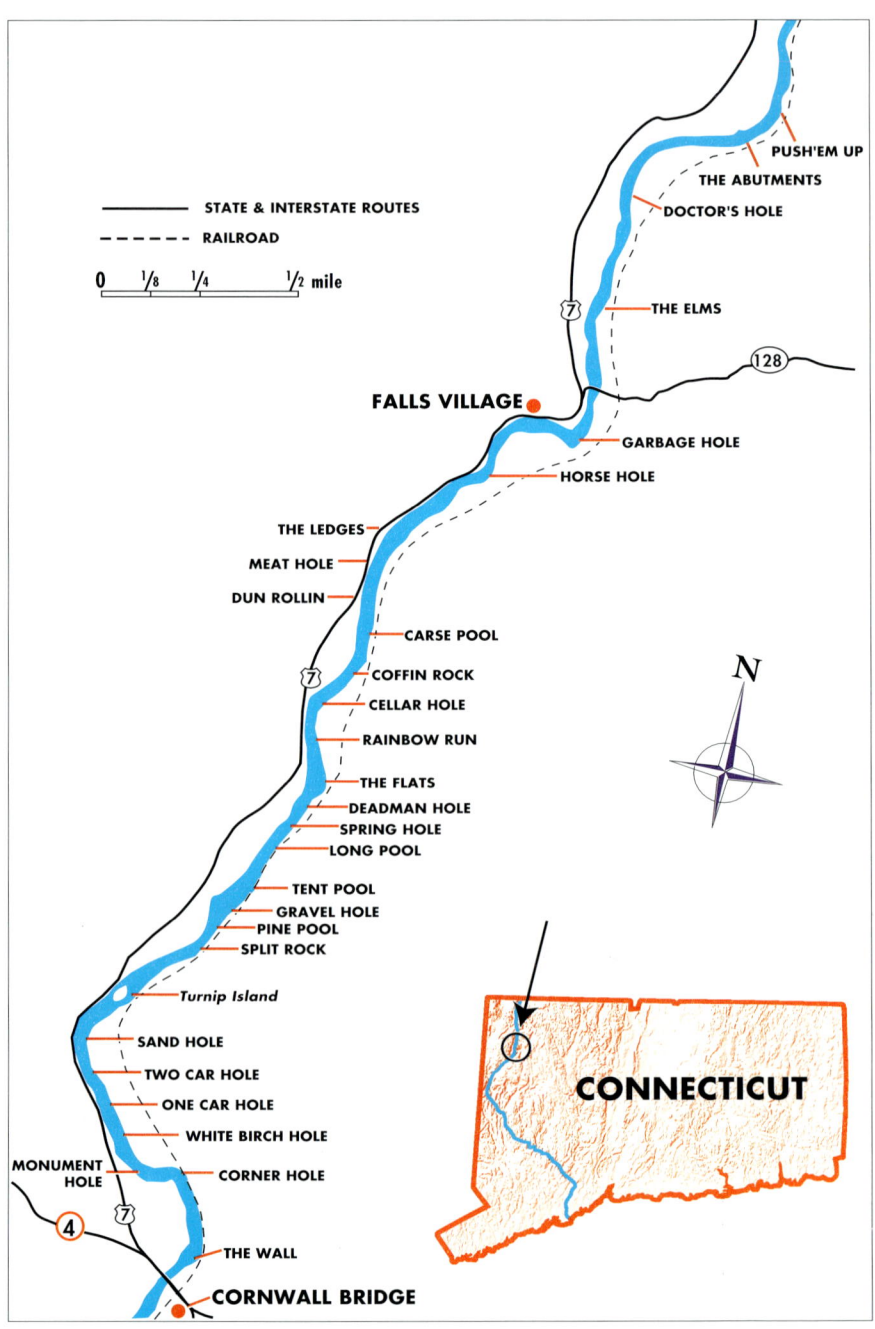

Introduction

Imagine brown and rainbow trout up to 20 inches rising to heavy insect hatches on a breathtakingly beautiful stream. Imagine that these trout are wild in the sense that they have lived and grown in the river for years. Montana? No, it's the Housatonic River in Connecticut.

The section of the Housatonic River that is of the most importance to trout fishermen is the Trout Management Area (TMA). This roughly 10-mile stretch runs between the towns of Cornwall and Sharon, Connecticut along Route 7. The bottom 3.5 miles is fly-fishing-only and the upper section is open to all forms of angling. The entire TMA is catch-and-release. The section directly below the TMA's southern border (the Route 4 bridge) is also excellent trout water for about another 10 miles all the way to the town of Kent. Even though the area below the TMA is not stocked by the state of Connecticut, it is stocked by private groups and there is a wild-trout population.

During the 1970s, polychlorinated biphenyls (PCBs) were discovered in the Housatonic. This carcinogen caused the state of Connecticut to suspend stocking during the 1980 fishing season. The governor of the state, Ella Grasso, actually issued the order at the last minute—the stocking trucks were on their way to the river and had to be turned around. The nature of the Housatonic as a trout river was about to be dramatically changed.

Fishermen spearheaded by the Housatonic Fly Fishermen's Association (HFFA) sued the state and demanded a return of the stocking program. The fishermen won the battle—the court ordered the state to stock the river and make the prime trout water a trout management area with catch-and-release regulations starting in 1981. The state Department of Environmental Protection (DEP) studied the trout yearly until the late 1980s under the new regulations. The results were amazing: survival rates of 40 percent and growth rates of 3.5 inches per year, and numbers that rival some Montana rivers. The reason for these great numbers is that the Housatonic is a rich stream in terms of aquatic insects and trout habitat. The hatches on the Hous rival any in the east.

If the Housatonic had one problem limiting its potential as a trout river it was the fact that during some summers the river would become so warm the trout would pool up at the mouths of the tributaries. New flow releases agreed to by the Falls Village hydroelectric dam operator, Northeast Utilities, in the summer of 1996, promise to help relieve the thermal problem and the future once again looks bright for the Housatonic trout.

Prolific hatches and big fussy trout can lead to frustrating days on the river. However, an angler who is aware of the hatches and how to fish them will be richly rewarded. This guide was written to help anglers learn about the hatches and the tactics that have worked for me for over 18 years. Hatches of course don't happen all the time, or even most of the time, but the fish tend to become most difficult during hatches because they can afford to become selective. How to handle those non-hatch periods will also be discussed since they can occur up to 90 percent of the time.

This book will not be a pool-by-pool guide–the HFFA has a excellent guide to fishing many of the pools on the river. Rather, this book is a practical guide that will help the angler wherever he or she is on the river because the flies and tactics are relevant to the whole river. The Housatonic is a classic riffle-and-pool type of stream, one pool fishes much like every other. Learn to fish one well and the river will open her treasures to you.

This book also assumes that the reader is not a novice fisherman. It assumes you are an angler seeking specific information on how to fish the river and its hatches. There will be no long discussions of fly casting, hooking and playing trout, or the life cycle of the insects. Such information can be found in many excellent books on the subject.

Finally, a bit of philosophy from Woody Allen who once said that "80 percent of life is about showing up." Lou Tabory in his excellent book, *Inshore Fly Fishing* said it differently when he stated "nothing beats time on the water." It's all the same. If you want to be a better fisherman, read as much as you can, practice your casting, but remember that nothing beats time on the water. Nothing.

Housatonic River Outfitters Fly Shop.

Chapter One
EQUIPMENT

Fly Rods

It seems as if everyone has an opinion about fly rods. I will tell you what I have found works for me on the Housatonic. Just remember not to get too carried away with the latest high-tech fly rod, a super fast rod that you can cast a country mile is not necessarily what you need. A medium to medium-fast action is usually the best choice for trout fishing since most trout are caught at ranges up to about 35 or 40 feet. The slightly slower actions are a lot more pleasant to cast and, at least for me, are more accurate and present the fly with more delicacy.

I prefer rods of 8 1/2 feet to 9 feet for most of my fishing. The Housatonic is a large open river so save your shorter rods for the tributaries. The longer length is very handy when nymph fishing as it allows you to mend your line and control your drift to a much greater degree. The longer length handles the wind with a bit more ease, also.

For the overwhelming majority of my trout fishing, I use a 4-weight. I find that this is the best compromise between delicacy and power. The 2-weight is fun to use when the river is low and the flies are small, but if the wind comes up you will wish you had something else. Any time the river is high, a 5- or 6-weight rod is a good choice. The heavier weight also handles streamers and weighted nymphs with more authority.

I use double-taper lines for all of my trout fishing. At the shorter distances that trout are fished for, I find the double-tapers work at least as well as the weight-forward lines. In addition, double-taper lines roll cast better, something you appreciate when you need it. And considering that you can reverse a double-taper and get twice the use out of it versus a weight-forward, swings the decision to double-taper for me, especially in light of the prices of premium lines. Buying a double-taper, in effect, gives you two fly lines for the price of one.

Waders

Stocking-foot waders are much preferred for the Housatonic over boot-foot waders. The bottom of the river is one mass of rocks and boulders making wading a tricky business. A wading fisherman must move over and around large rocks all day. Stocking-foot waders with their felt wading shoe, provide the maneuverability and feel to negotiate the river bottom with confidence. Boot foots are just too cumbersome. In addition, your waders should be as non-restrictive as possible, otherwise all the knee lifts will leave you exhausted by the end of the day. Neoprenes, fly-weights, and the new breathable waders are all good choices.

Wading Staffs

I don't use a wading staff for a couple of reasons. First, they always tend to get in the way, and second, they are noisy. Often, I have heard a fly fisherman approach from the klink of his wading staff alone as it sounded along the bottom. Imagine what the fish must be thinking. The noise issue bothers me (and the trout the most) since I usually cover a lot of ground. I have tried different "stoppers" on the bottom of the staff, but they usually come off in short order. So, for the time being, I am not using a wading staff. Having said that, let me say that if you are new to the river, consider a wading staff a necessity until you know the river better. And once you are familiar with the river, if you feel more comfortable and secure with a staff, by all means use it. Safety first.

Wading is always tricky business on the Housatonic. Be especially careful in early spring.

Nets

Nets are another item I don't use. I have found that it is much easier and quicker to release a fish without a net. Simply reach down the tippet to the fly and twist off or use your forceps to remove the hook. Of course, barbless hooks are a big help here. The fish is not touched and is released very quickly. I guarantee you that a trout can be landed and released in this manner much quicker than with a net and that means the fish has a much better chance at survival. It also gets you back to fishing much sooner. If you want to take a picture, you can place your hand under the fish and with the weight balanced, you can lift the fish out of the water for a quick shot. I have done this with many fish over 20 inches and they have remained perfectly still. The only time I would consider using a net is when fishing with 7X–all tippets stronger than 7X will easily hold for the hand release. If you must use a net, use one with a soft mesh bag of cotton. The catch-and-release net is a good one or tie a knot in your net to create a shallow net which will facilitate the release.

Leaders

The leader that I have been using for the past few seasons is the leader Gary Borger calls the Uni-Body Leader in his classic book *Presentation*. The beauty of this leader is that it is easy to tie and handles nymphs and dries equally well. At one time, I would change leaders back and forth for nymphs and dries—no more. The formula for the Uni-Body is:

Length	Size
4 feet	.020 (usually Maxima Chameleon)
1 foot	.013 (usually Maxima Chameleon)
4 feet	.010

This is the basic leader. To fish nymphs, add a tippet of 6 to 8 inches of 2X, 3X, 4X, or 5X. The leader will be 9 1/2 feet and can handle split shot and an indicator, and still turn over beautifully. I put the strike indicator, usually yarn, on the one-foot section of .013 with an overhand knot. The split shot should be put on the tippet section. I usually fish two nymphs and put the split shot between the two flies.

For dries, the tippet section of 3X, 4X, or 5X is 2 to 4 feet. If you want to fish 6X or 7X, add one foot to the end of the 4X. This leader will be between 11 and 14 feet. Use the longer lengths for tough spring creek conditions and the shorter lengths for windy conditions. This leader has worked great on the Housatonic as well as in Montana.

I attach the tippets to the basic leader with loops. I put a surgeon's loop in the end of both the basic leader and the tippet and loop them together. This allows for quick changes of tippet and makes switching back and forth between nymphs and dries quite easy.

Chapter Two
DAM RELEASES

It's one of those absolutely great Housatonic mornings. The river is down and the green caddis are hatching and the trout are responding with gusto. The dogwoods and apple trees are in bloom and the rest of the hardwoods have the delicate light green color of newly unfurled leaves. Two fly fishermen new to the river are in Two Car Hole having the time of their lives catching fat Housy browns. It's one of those days when everyone has a smile on their face. During a lull, at 10:30, they decide to take a break and get some breakfast in town. When they return at 11:30 and start to put their waders on, the river comes up and the fishing shuts down. They ask me how it was while they were gone, eyes pleading for me to say it was slow—I have to tell them the truth, it was great. Since they can't stay until the evening, their fishing is done for the day. Sounds crazy but it's a true story and it happens all the time.

Understanding the impact of the dam releases from the hydroelectric facility at Falls Village and its relation to the fishing is absolutely vital. No other single factor has a bigger effect on the fishing and the catching.

The Falls Village dam is about 7 miles upstream from the beginning of the Trout Management Area (TMA). The impoundment behind the dam is relatively shallow reaching a maximum depth of about 12 feet. Therefore, there is no cooling of the water behind the dam as there is behind some of the famous tailwaters such as the Bighorn and Missouri rivers. In addition, the dam generates electricity by drawing water through as many as three turbines one or more times a day.

The Falls Village Hydroelectric Facility was built in 1914. Power generation from this dam causes water level fluctuations downstream in the TMA.

What this means to a downstream angler is that usually in the course of a day's fishing, the river will come up at some point and make fishing difficult if not dangerous. In most cases, the water will come up at midday and recede before the evening rise. This arrangement allows the power company, Northeast Utilities (NU) to generate, the paddlers to float the river during the afternoons, and allows the fishermen low water in the mornings and evenings when the fishing is normally the best.

NU provides a hot line with the water release schedule for the following day, usually updated by 3 p.m. The NU number is (1-888-417-4837). Don't leave home without calling. Rising water from the Falls Village dam takes approximately 2.5 hours to reach the top of the TMA and another 1.5 hours to reach the bottom of the TMA. For example, if NU's recording states that the morning release will be at 10:00 a.m., and you are fishing near the bottom of the TMA, you can expect to see rising water about 2 p.m. Some fishermen, if they are fishing the upper end, will get in their cars as the water starts to rise and go to the lower sections of the TMA to get in an extra hour or so of fishing. On the drop, the waters seem to recede more slowly than they came up. For instance, if NU shuts down at 2 p.m., it takes longer than the 2.5 hours for the water to recede to its normal shutdown level, figure on 3.5 hours.

Heavy spring rains and snow runoff can cause early season flooding on the river. Only the foolhardy venture forth.

When NU gives the water release schedule for a day, they will normally give the time of release along with the units or generators they will be bringing on-line. NU has three generators at Falls Village. Each unit has the capacity to release 600 cubic feet per second (cfs). For example, if NU states they are releasing three units or generators, you can expect up to 1800 cfs. During high-water periods such as the early spring, water will spill over the dam raising the cfs as high as 6000 cfs (one reason to always call NU before going to the river). During shutdown periods, NU will be "ponding" water behind the dam in order to build up for the next release. During shutdown, the cfs of the release is actually "leakage" from the dam–presently about 150 cfs. Discussions are underway to raise this to about 330 cfs in the future, a number that the state's Department of Fisheries studies indicate is the proper minimum flow for this river.

What do all these cfs numbers mean to the fishing? In general, the lower the better, especially for dry-fly fishing. Shutdown provides easy wading and great access to all parts of the river. At this level, the fish will tend to congregate in the deeper holes, look for fish at the top of pools where there may be a depression. During a good hatch, I have seen as many as 100 heads rising in such a spot. The fishing can be very exacting, however, much like spring-creek fishing. Delicate casts, long leaders, and careful approaches are needed to score well. Be forewarned–it's not for the faint of heart–many large fish rising in a relatively small area can raise your blood pressure to a dangerous level.

One unit equates to about 600 cfs and the fish will be much more spread out. Wading is not easy at this level, but equipped with a wading staff and felt soles, an experienced wader should not have too much trouble. One unit provides excellent fishing both dry and wet. Nymph fishing is best at this level. Spotting rising fish is more difficult, but the fish tend to be less selective due to the fact that they have more water over their backs. Casting blindly to likely spots will also pay off now.

At two units, or up to 1200 cfs, the fishing is usually marginal but can, when the conditions are right, be very good. If the river has been consistently high for some time, the fish get adjusted to the high water and actually feed on the surface fairly well, particularly if the river is somewhat clear. The best part is that if you do find them rising, the trout will not be super selective. When the river rises to 1200 cfs rather quickly during a release, the fish usually go down but there are always exceptions. Wading is very tough at this level and only the foolhardy venture out more than a few feet from shore. Fish the edges, the fish will be there if they are not pushed off the bank by a careless fisherman. Some excellent high-water spots are the Wall, Sand Hole, and the Gravel Hole. Above 2 units the fishing is usually very difficult even for Housy veterans. Try the tributaries like Furnace Brook and Mill Brook which have native populations as well as stocked fish.

The river can surprise though. One late November afternoon I stopped at Sand Hole with the river running at about 2000 cfs and the air temperature near 40 degrees. As I casually walked the bank, I noticed numerous trout rising along the edge of the flow. I quickly scrambled back to the car, found the fly rod (always prepared), and had a memorable day fishing Griffith's Gnats to midging trout.

The seasons can have a large impact on the flow regimes as well. During early spring, depending on the snowpack and the spring rains, the river is usually running high and the normal pond and release procedure cannot be accomplished because of the excess water coming over the Falls Village dam. As the trees leaf out and the air temperatures rise, the river drops and Falls Village goes onto the normal schedule of midday releases with its low water in the mornings and evenings. This folds in perfectly with the bulk of Housatonic mayfly and caddis hatches which occur primarily during May and June. The receding waters in the evening drop to low enough levels to provide excellent evening fishing.

Due to the fact that water temperatures can be elevated during late June, July, and August–stressing the trout–special flow regimes are now in effect. An air-water model has been developed that predicts downstream temperatures in the thermal refuges at different cfs releases. During the summer months, NU will consult the air-water model daily and release water at levels to protect the refuges. For instance, if water temperatures are predicted to reach above 75 degrees in these thermal refuges with a 600 cfs release, NU will decrease the amount of release until the air-water model predicts a downstream temperature of 75 or less. This is done in order to protect the trout in the thermal refuges from large slugs of warm water overrunning the sanctuaries. If water temperatures are not predicted to exceed 75 degrees on a given day in the refuges, normal 2 unit midday releases can be expected if there is enough water in the system. These special summer flow regimes, although not perfect, have given the Hous' trout fishery a major boost in the arm. During hot, dry summers, fishkills as high as 80 percent would plague the river. Due to the cooperation between NU and the various fishing organizations and the state's DEP, the new flow schedule based on the air-water model was worked out and now the future of the trout fishery in the Hous is indeed bright.

As always, call NU's number to verify the release schedule. If NU is on the modified summer schedule of releasing 350 cfs to protect the trout, forget about fishing for trout. All of the trout will be in the thermal refuges and it is illegal to fish within 100 feet of the tributaries during the period of June 15 through August 31. Smallmouth bass fishing, however, can be outrageous during a hot, dry period.

After September 15th, the release schedule calls for no generation between 8 a.m. and 4 p.m. on the "fishing days" of Monday, Friday, and Sunday. Generation of two units starts at 10 a.m. on the "paddling days" of Tuesday, Wednesday, Thursday, and Saturday. This different pattern for different days allows the paddlers and fishermen to share the river by

An angler approaches The Birches from the east side of the river. Fishing from the opposite side of the river from the road can be very effective.

alternating their use throughout the fall season. Later in the fall, from October 16th through November 15th, there is no generation between 8 a.m. and 4 p.m. all days of the week. This schedule was worked out by members of HFFA and representatives from NU and the paddlers in order to provide some fishing days with low water in the afternoons when the olives hatch.

As a general rule, the size of the artificial flies used can increase as the water level increases. For example, during shutdown periods when the river is running anywhere from 150-350 cfs, large flies rarely work well. As the cfs increases up towards 1200 or even 1800 cfs, the same trout will aggressively take large sizes such as 10s and 12s. In October, when both the size 20 and 28 olives are on the water with the size 10 *Isonychias*, for instance, I fish the *Isonychias* when the river is up and the olives when the river is low. Fishing small flies when the river is high is a tough game—one popular spot for fall olives during high water is the Wall where there always seem to be rising fish in the long, flat runs. I prefer to tie on a *Isonychia* imitation during those high water times and fish the pockets and edges. I am rarely disappointed.

The Housatonic is not a dangerous river if you pay attention. When the river does rise, it does so slowly and subtly. And it is that slow rise that can get a visiting angler in trouble because he may not be aware of the rise until he attempts to re-cross the river. First of all, call the NU number before leaving home to be aware of when the river is "supposed" to come up. I say supposed to because they do occasionally change the schedule due to power demands or upstream thunderstorms. Be constantly alert to clues of rising water while fishing such as a change in river noise or a sudden drop in rising fish, canoes spotted upstream, or other anglers heading for shore. If you suspect rising water, the acid test is to check a rock barely above water and if it submerges, then head for shore immediately. Also, be aware that on the east side of the river, railroad tracks parallel the river the entire length of the TMA. Therefore, if you do get stranded on the east side of the river and need to get to the west side where your car most likely is, follow the tracks to a bridge and cross over. Don't lose your head and try to cross the river after waiting too long to cross over. The train tracks may be a long walk but at least you will arrive alive. And if you pay attention and get out early, you will never have to make that long walk—I never have.

Talks are underway between the Federal Energy Regulatory Commission (FERC) and NU concerning the relicencing of the Falls Village dam due in the year 2001. Natural flow or run of the river is a possibility for the TMA in the future. At a bare minimum, natural flow in the summer would relieve the bulk of the river's temperature problems. If natural flow becomes a reality year-round on the Hous, the fishing information in the chapter would remain valuable. The fishing approaches and tactics will always be valid for the cfs levels regardless of releases from the dam. Natural flow would have the advantage of allowing the fish to settle down and establish a set feeding pattern. Dry-fly fishing would be much improved. The potential certainly exists that under natural flow the Hous could reach its destiny as one of the great trout rivers in the United States.

Chapter Three
THE HATCHES AND HOW TO FISH THEM

The Housatonic is a very rich tailwater river with many of the characteristics of a spring creek. The limestone ridge that runs through the car racing town of Lime Rock adds its nutrients to the Housatonic which raises the pH level into the 7.5 range, which is quite a good number for a freestone stream. The richness of the stream coupled with the stream's bottom of large and small rocks with some gravel provides a perfect habitat for aquatic insects. Hatches on the Housatonic can be as prolific and diverse as any in the East.

A 10-mile section of the Housatonic became a catch-and-release area or Trout Management Area (TMA) in 1980. The survival and growth rate exhibited by the Housatonic trout under these catch-and-release regulations was phenomenal. Holdover trout over 16 inches are not uncommon. As word of the success of the TMA spread by word of mouth and through the angling press, the crowds on the river have increased. As a result, knowledge of the river's hatches and how to fish them is vital to consistent angling success.

This chapter is organized by super hatches first, followed by the other important mayfly and caddis hatches. The final sections deal with the miscellaneous trout foods such as terrestrials and scuds.

Super Hatches

Doug Swisher and Carl Richards in their classic *Selective Trout* used the term "Super Hatch" to refer to the most productive hatches. They felt that 80 percent of all fly fishing to rising trout would be to these insects. In my mind, a hatch has to meet certain criteria in order to qualify as a super hatch. These criteria are:

1. Consistency
The hatch must be solid from year to year–not having blizzard hatches one year and being invisible the next.

2. Acceptance
A large hatch that trout ignore is not a super hatch. Examples of good hatches in numbers on the Hous that are not super hatches are the Housatonic Quill (*Ephoron leukon*) and the Alder (*Macronema zebratum*), actually a size 12 caddis. Both of these insects would make most people's lists but not mine because the water temperatures when they emerge, in August and June, are usually in the mid to upper 70s–too high for good trout fishing.

3. Duration
A super hatch should last for at least two weeks. The brown drake spinner

falls can be awesome and provide some fast fishing but they rarely last more than two or three days.

4. Concentrations

A super hatch will be concentrated during at least one stage in order to bring the numbers of trout up. An example of a lack of large numbers at one time is the *Isonychia* hatch which hatches in August and September. The *Isonychia* is a large mayfly and the trout do love them but it is rare on the Hous to see numerous duns on the water at one time and I have never witnessed a large spinner fall.

5. Availability

At some stage of emergence or during the spinner fall, the insect should be available and vulnerable to the trout in good numbers. Most of the caddis hatches on the Hous do not provide good dry-fly fishing during the emergence with one exception—the green caddis hatch. Otherwise, the best caddis fishing is during the egg-laying flights in the mornings and evenings— a productive but spotty situation.

So there you have it, my definition of a super hatch. I believe that there are four super hatches on the Housatonic: three mayflies and a caddis. One of the East's premier spring hatches is the first super hatch, the Hendrickson.

Hendricksons

The first of the four super hatches occurs during the last half of April and is of course the Hendricksons (*Ephemerella subvaria*). When the magnolias and forsythias are in full bloom in Connecticut, about the 17th of April, the first of the Hendricksons will emerge. The hatch typically lasts about two weeks but can last weeks longer and often provides some of the best fishing of the year. The first few days of the hatch seem to produce the most intense hatches but the best fishing occurs during the end of the two-week cycle to

Playing a nice trout.

the spinner falls. The hatches begin around 2:00 p.m. and last until 5:00 p.m. with the spinners taking over until dark. I have seen good hatches as early as 9:30 a.m. on very warm days during low water conditions; unfortunately it's a rare situation on the Hous in April.

Typically, the river will be running at two units during the hatch which means that the fish will take the duns very aggressively—if at all. On windy days, which are the norm during this time of year, the trout will indicate their presence by slashing at the duns much in the manner of a caddis rise. Sparkle Duns in size 12 or 14 are very effective and I prefer to use the male reddish-brown coloring for the body color. If the fish are on the emergers, then the Rabbit Foot Emerger in sizes 12 and 14 is all you need.

The real key to this hatch on the Hous is the spinner falls. The hatches are usually outstanding but the trout's reaction to the dun can range from indifference to eager acceptance depending on the year and the conditions (water levels, temperature, weather). The spinners are usually money in the bank. The spinner falls become increasingly important as the hatch progresses into the second and even third week. This is because

*Female Hendrickson dun (*Ephemeralla subvaria*)*

the hatches after the first week are sparse and spread out over the whole day, giving the trout few opportunities to "get on station." They quickly learn, however, that the spinners are a concentrated and vulnerable meal available during the last hour or so of daylight. Keep in mind, also, that on cloudy days the spinner falls will start much earlier and may overlap the emergence. During these overlap situations, fish both the Sparkle Dun and the spinner. A size 12 or 14 Rusty Spinner tied with either poly or hackle spent wings is the standard spinner pattern. In addition, try the Sparkle Duns during the spinner fall since many of the spinners will come down to the water with their wings up and the Sparkle Dun has the added advantage of being easier to see than the flush-riding spinner.

When fishing the spinner in the evening, the best strategy is to fish the tail-out of pools where the trout will be looking for the spinners. It is important to look for flat areas, with a minimum of chop during high water conditions, in order to spot the fish rising in the fading light. The fish will rise, with the classic head and tail rise, and will not move very far for a spinner, so your casts must be right on. Another effective approach is to carefully walk the bank looking for bank-feeders that will move in if the water level is two units or more. Walk slowly up the bank but do try to cover as much ground as possible. I have caught more fish over 16 inches during Hendrickson hatches than any other single hatch and the beauty is that every fish you catch is a holdover—the Hous does not usually receive any stockings until mid-May.

Green Caddis

The second super hatch is the green caddis hatch which appears around the 15th of May and lasts two weeks. The river is coming alive with dogwoods and apple trees in bloom and turkeys and Canada geese in their mating rituals. The air and water temperatures are usually ideal for fly fishing and these days in late May can be some of the most memorable of the year.

The green caddis is about a size 16 although there is some variation in size between 14 and 18 with the size 18 being the best pattern size for super-selective fish. The green caddis has tan wings and a bright green body with some having a grayish cast to the green of the body perhaps related to the amount of time they have been exposed to the air. The hatch starts around 9:00 a.m. and continues until about noon. This caddis hatch is unusual in that the caddis hatch and "motorboat" around on the surface for quite a while before taking off. Some of the caddis float down the river as quietly and serenely as a mayfly. In short, this caddis hatch acts more like a mayfly hatch than the normal caddis hatch in which the hatching caddis are not very available to the trout on the surface. All of this "uncaddis-like" behavior means that the trout will move into position and feed on the green caddis with great relish.

The river is home to many Canada geese. Low-flying formations moving upstream can fly very low to the surface of the river causing midstream anglers to duck.

During good years, the river will be in the shutdown mode during the morning hours when this hatch is on. The best approach is to get to the stream about 8:30 a.m. and get into position at the tail of a run. Fishing a caddis larva or Bead-head Caddis in the early morning hours before the hatch can be very productive. Once the hatch starts it is usually wise to wait, before you commence casting, until the trout really get on the skittering adults. The best patterns are the Elk Wing Caddis, Henryville and Green Caddis in sizes 16 and 18.

The key to this hatch is to cover as much water as possible. As you fish over a pod of fish, the fishing will initially be very good but will get tougher and tougher as time goes on. At this point it is a good idea to change flies and fly design, for instance from a Elk Wing Caddis to a Henryville. This minor tactic will usually be good for another fish or two but that is about all. It is definitely more efficient to move on because there will be fish rising all over the river. It is very difficult to leave rising fish but to maximize your opportunities you must.

The green caddis is one of the best hatches to fish the pocket waters.

During May, the trout will be spread out over the entire river as water temperatures are in the 60s. If the river is low, try a morning of what I call "pocket picking." Approach each pocket carefully and slowly from below and determine exactly where the trout are rising within that pocket. The fish in these pocket areas are usually not as shy as the trout in the pools simply because they do not receive anywhere near the fishing pressure. There will usually be trout near the tail and also at the head depending on the size of the pocket. Check the tail first and watch the fish feed for awhile before making the cast in order to determine the trout's feeding rhythm and from what direction he is expecting his food. Cast to individual fish always, working your way from the tail to the head. The size of the fish in these pockets will amaze you. The best part of "pocket picking" is that the fishing is usually fast and you won't have much competition.

As the days and evenings warm toward the end of May, the returning caddis adults become important in the evenings. These ovipositing caddis will lay their eggs and become available to the trout once again. During these late May evenings there will be many mayfly hatches you will have to contend with for the trouts' attention, but many times they will take the most vulnerable insect. That insect usually is the spent caddis. For this situation, I fish the Mike Lawson's Spent Partridge Caddis and usually score very well.

Brown trout.

Sulphurs

The third super hatch is the sulphurs (*Ephemerella dorothea*) sometimes referred to as the pale evening dun. This hatch starts during the last week of May and continues into the later part of June with the peak activity usually around the first week of June. The dun is a size 16 or 18 and ranges in color from a creamy white to a pale yellow with tinges of orange near the thorax. The hatches and spinner falls occur during the last hour or so of daylight and quite often last well past sunset.

The trout show a definite preference to emergers during this hatch. The Rabbit Foot Emerger in size 16 or the Emerger in size 16 or 18 are extremely effective. The fur from a snowshoe rabbit's hind foot is one of those magical materials like peacock herl or pheasant tail herl that, when incorporated into an artificial, makes it that much more effective. Since Art Lee's article in *Fly Fisherman*, "The Usual With a Twist," I have fished various usual-type emergers for the sulphur hatch with outstanding success. My favorite variation is a dark brown body with no tail and an orange-gold rabbit foot wing colored with a Pantone pen and tied in Compara-dun style. This emerger pattern is also very effective for the pale morning duns (PMD) found on western waters. The fly floats on the wing with the back end of the fly underwater which is the general configuration of an emerging dun. One July morning during a PMD hatch on the Madison River in Montana, the orange-gold emerger caught a 3 1/2-pound brown that took the fly on the first float after refusing numerous other patterns.

The Ed Shenk sulphur pattern is my favorite dun imitation. Ed's Sulphur Dun is tied with a cream body and an orange thorax and tied with two hackles over the thorax and spread out so the orange shows through. Dun imitations work best when there are few duns on the water–particularly during the tail end of the hatch. Work your way upstream covering as much water as possible and cast to the few trout that are still on the duns. Spinner falls can be very important on the Housatonic just as dark approaches and some trout will become selective to the spinners. As a result, carry size 16 and 18 Rusty Spinners.

A very effective technique at dusk is to fish two flies, one effective combination is a spinner and a dun. The cream-colored dun serves as the strike indicator. The tippet for the second fly can be attached to the bend of the first fly with a cinch knot. In this way you will be able to determine whether

Dun Rollin pool is the beginning of the fly-fishing-only water. The fly area continues downstream to the Route 4/7 bridge.

the fish are on the spinner or the dun. Of course, other combinations can be made, such as a dun and a Pheasant Tail Nymph. The Pheasant Tail Nymph is an excellent representation of the *Ephemerella* nymphs. One early June evening over 15 years ago, I ran into photographer Dale Spartus near the state-run campground. Dale was having a great time fishing a caddis pupa trailing a sulphur dun. Most of the fish he caught that night fell to the caddis pupa but the largest fish, a healthy 18-inch brown, was caught on the sulphur dun.

Blue-winged Olive (BWO)

The last of the super hatches is the BWO which occurs all season long but is particularly concentrated during the fall. The BWOs range in size from a 20 to 28 and are made up of two different insects. The most common is the former *Pseudocloeon*, now *Baetis* or *Acentrella,* which ranges from a size 24 to 28. In addition, on some days, a larger *Baetis* hatch in the 20-22 range. The BWOs hatch in the afternoons but will hatch all day long during periods of overcast. The hatches begin in earnest in mid-September and last well into November. The peak of the hatch coincides with the peak of the foliage season usually near Columbus Day weekend in October. At that time of year, the Housatonic Valley will be ablaze in color, the roads buzzing with leaf peeping tourists and the trout delicately sipping BWOs in the quiet runs.

Without a doubt, the BWOs are the most frustrating of the four super hatches. Trout will porpoise rise practically in your waders and yet refuse all the standard offerings. My first visits to the river and its BWO hatches were typical. I would arrive in the early afternoon to a river with fish rising like it was feeding time at the hatchery. With shaking hands I would rig up and dash into the river figuring that I finally was at the right place at the right time. But hours later I would wade ashore with frozen feet and little to show for my efforts. Then one day while sitting dejectedly on a midstream rock I saw a fly fisherman working his way towards me catching numerous trout along the way. I knew him only as Swede, then a Vice President of HFFA and a devout trout bum. Swede showed me his poly-wing BWO and invited me to fish the river with him. The world of BWO fishing in the fall opened up to me.

The poly BWO is tied in sizes 20-28 with 24 being the most useful. I avoid hooks smaller than 24 since hooking and holding trout on hooks smaller than 24 is difficult at best. The poly BWO has split tails, green or olive body (usually of thread) and a dun or white polywing, a parachute dun hackle is optional. This fly should be fished on a long 7X tippet in order to eliminate as much drag as possible. Downstream floats in the trouts' precise feeding lane are very effective. The trout stay just under the surface during a good hatch, so they have a small window and therefore your casts must be right on. The poly-wing post can be cut down onstream to form an emerger as the trout many times will show a preference for the emergers. My favorite emerger is a size 20 Pheasant Tail Nymph with a ball of gray poly on top to form a floating nymph.

As effective as the emerger and the dun are, frequently that is not what the trout are looking for. Many times the best trout will be feeding on the

Ralph Hasnosi in Cellar Hole. Convenient access and good blue-winged olive hatches contribute to Cellar Hole's popularity.

swimming BWO nymphs as they work their way to the surface to hatch. Use a tiny yarn strike indicator about two to three feet from the fly and a micro-shot 12 inches from a size 20 nymph. Keep the strike indicator as small as possible, about the size of a pea, in order not to spook the trout. The most effective nymphs are the Pheasant Tail, RS2, and peacock herl simply tied to the hook. Make your casts slightly upstream of visibly rising fish and watch that strike indicator closely. This is without a doubt the most effective way to take trout during the BWO hatch. It is especially satisfying to catch trout that have spurned your dun and emerger patterns, in this manner.

Spinners will sometimes be important, especially when they overlap with the beginning of the hatch. Many of the larger trout key in on the spinners. A size 24 Rusty Spinner is all you need.

Terrestrials can be an ace in the hole during BWO hatches. A small ant, or my personal favorite, a size 14 beetle, will on occasion produce banner days. One drizzly October afternoon, over 30 trout took a beetle at the Wall, home of some of the most selective trout on the river. The next day under identical conditions, the fly was ignored–go figure.

Low river flows are critical to good BWO fishing. The HFFA has worked out an agreement with Northeast Utilities (NU) to provide low water conditions during the afternoons in the fall. The agreement has opened the window of good fall fishing on the river. When NU has too much water to hold back, the key is to locate those areas on the river that have long, flat glides with a minimum of chop. The Wall and Sand Hole are two popular high-water spots.

Other Hatches

The Housatonic is a very rich river with good mayfly hatches and even better caddis hatches. The first main hatches of the year are the Hendrickson and green caddis hatches but they are soon followed by the late May/early-June smorgasbord.

Mayflies

Cream Mayflies

In late May, the gray fox (*Stenonema fuscum*) and the light Cahill (*Stenonema ithaca* and *canadense*) hatch on warm evenings. These are large insects averaging around a size 12. These mayflies usually hatch sporadically during the day and evening. The larger holdover brown trout seem reluctant to take these large mayflies except under the cover of darkness or near darkness. Since these mayflies are large and obvious, most fly fishermen key in

When the foliage is at its peak, the olive hatches also peak.
This scene is the area above the Abutments pool.

on them much more than the trout do. Many times I have observed these stately and beautiful duns sailing past me and down the pool and around the bend, untouched by the trout. The key here is, as always, to observe the trout and their feeding. Frequently, at this time of year, the trout will be feeding on caddis and emerging caddis pupae, ignoring the high-floating cream duns. As darkness approaches, however, the game will usually change. The larger fish will move out and feed on the cream duns; the White Wulff is one of my favorites at this time. The spinner falls are always important and a size 12-14 Cream Spinner will take many fish at dusk. The two-fly combo of the White Wulff with a trailing spinner is a particularly good one to try as darkness sets in and the bats start their nightly flyovers.

March Browns

The March brown (*Stenonema vicarium*) hatches in late May usually right after the gray fox. The March brown is a beautiful insect with tannish body and mottled brown wings and is about a size 10. The comments concerning the cream mayflies applies for the March brown with the exception of the fly pattern. Any of the standard March brown patterns will work and the

Rusty Spinner in size 12 is deadly during a spinner fall. Prior to the hatch of any of the *Stenonema* insects, a size 12 March brown nymph fished on the bottom will prove very rewarding.

Brown Drakes

The brown drake (*Ephemera simulans*) is a large insect represented by a size 8 hook and measuring 11 to 14mm long (that's big). The mayflies hatch and fly to the underside of the leaves along the banks. If you are wondering if the brown drakes are about, check the foliage along the stream, especially above the covered bridge. The duns are easily recognized by their size and their mottled wings and can be distinguished from the March brown which has two tails to the brown drake's three. These hatches can be very heavy but are usually very short in duration–about 3-4 days. The hatches occur at the very end of May or during the first few days of June. A Sparkle Dun with a chocolate brown body or a parachute with a deer wing will take fish during this hatch. The spinner flights in the evenings can be downright awesome. Huge flights will suddenly form up above treetop level as dusk approaches and just as

Sand Hole on an early summer day. Good caddis and mayfly hatches and comfortable wading can be found in this pool.

suddenly disappear. My suspicion is that a lot of the spinners come down at night but I have witnessed spinner falls at dusk and it is not a sight one soon forgets. Since most of the spinners land with their wings up, I fish the dun patterns right through the spinner fall. The brown drake's sister hatch, the green drake (*Ephemera guttulata*), does appear on some sections of the river. The HFFA introduced the green drake nymphs to the river from Mill River in Hamden and it has been partially successful. I have seen the green drake's unmistakable spinner, the coffin fly, in the evening but the green drake is not yet an important hatch on the Hous.

Serratella deficiens

This insect does not have a common name that I know of other than "little dark blue quill." My research indicates that this insect is a *Serratella deficiens* although others refer to it as the *Ephemerella needhami*. In any event, the dun is a size 20 and has a dark brown-black body with dark gray wings. It hatches in June, in late morning, and the hatches will be particularly heavy on dark overcast days. This is one hatch that is overlooked by many fishermen but the trout show a definite preference to these small duns. Tiny sparkle duns or parachutes

Eastern green drake dun (Ephemera guttulata)

with a dark brown body imitate the dun. Many times the fish will be just starting to work on these duns as the water comes up at midday. Pay attention to the back eddies and areas near shore because oftentimes, with the water rising or already up, the fish will continue to feed on the tiny *deficiens* well into the early afternoon. The spinners return in the evening and are represented by a size 20 Rusty Spinner.

Housatonic Quill

Otherwise known as the white fly (*Ephoron leukon*), their hatches begin in the first week of August and last for about two weeks. In years when the water temperatures are below 70 in the evenings, this hatch can provide spectacular trout fishing. The dun will hatch just as dark approaches and, at the peak of the hatch, the flies will be so numerous that the term "blizzard hatch" is very appropriate. Much like the famous Trico hatches, the duns molt and return to the water as mature spinners within an hour or two. The surface of the river will be covered with these dead or dying spinners and the trout will have a feast. During these blanket hatches the fishing can be very difficult but the size 14 White Wulff and size 14 Cream Spinner will work as well as any imitation. Since this hatch starts right at dark, don't leave early. Many times the fishing will be the best an hour after dark and you will need a light to check the contents of your net to determine whether you have caught a trout or bass. Look for areas to fish where there is a smooth surface with some remaining light. You will learn to strike at what sounds like a rise near your fly and occasionally the pressure on your rod will tell you that you guessed right. The white fly will bring the smallmouths to the surface like no other hatch.

Isonychia

Isonychia bicolor and *sadleri* hatch from mid-July until the end of October. I have never witnessed a heavy hatch of this insect but have seen enough on the water, especially in August and September, to interest the trout. This is another hatch that seems to fish better when the water levels are high. During those times in the fall when the water levels are too elevated for good BWO fishing, try fishing a large Sparkle Dun, Adams, or EMBT, size

10 or 12, along the edges. If the water has been up more than a few days, the larger fish will move in toward shore and they relish the large *Isonychia* duns. The same general rule pertaining to all large duns definitely applies here: fish large imitations during high water and avoid them like the plague during low water because the trout certainly will. Nymph fishing with peacock imitations such as the Prince or the Scraggly can be deadly anytime of the day and is probably the best way to fish the *Isonychia* when the water is down. Fish the nymphs with a retrieve, rising them from the bottom in front of boulders and tailouts.

Caddis

The Housatonic is primarily a caddis river. The most consistent and dependable hatches all season long are caddis hatches.

One HFFA member and Yale student, Rodrigo Andrade, collected, during part of the 1983 season, 34 different species of caddisflies on the river. The caddis were identified by Dr. Downes, an MD and avid amateur entomologist from Branford, Connecticut. Someday all of the caddisflies may be identified but for now we can thank Dr. Downes for what we do know. Most of the caddisflies identified by Dr. Downes were from the *Hydropsyche* and *Cheumatopsyche* genus. Fortunately, in order to fish them effectively we need not know all the Latin. The following is a list of the more important caddis hatches on the river after the green caddis.

Alders

The alder (*Macronema zebratum*) or zebra caddis is one of the river's most famous hatches. Similar to the famous salmonfly hatches of the West or the green drake hatches of the Catskills, actually fishing to the hatch can disappoint. However, when the water levels and temperatures are right, the fishing can be spectacular.

The alder is a beautiful insect with tan wings with black markings and very long antennas. The size is a 12 and the body is dark brown to black. Alders will fly to the surrounding bushes once they hatch and on windy days will find themselves blown on the water much in the manner of grasshoppers during the "grasshopper winds" so common in the West. The alder population is heavier on the river above the covered bridge due to the denser foliage in that area. Alders are very erratic fliers and with their large size will drive trout mad with their wild antics on or near the surface. On many occasions I have seen very large trout jump completely out of the water in hot pursuit of an alder that was apparently flying out of control. The erratic flying of the alder is related to the egg-laying flights of the females.

Alders start appearing around the first week in June and last well into July and usually appear along with the much smaller black caddis. Patterns for the alder abound, with most incorporating peacock herl in the body. Well-mottled turkey quill is a good match for the wings and a brown hackle wound in the front finishes off an effective pattern. The King River Caddis in size 12 is one of my favorites. Imitating the prominent antennae with stripped hackle quills is a nice touch and can fool the selective feeder. This is one hatch that fishes better when the water is up from one to two units. I like to wade out from the bank (carefully) and cast back in toward shore where the trout will be looking up for alders falling from the bushes.

The alder (Macronema zebratum).

Pound the fly in rather hard, and don't be afraid to skitter it to imitate the behavior of the alder. If the water is too deep to get out to from shore, fish along the bank and under bushes with the same skittering cast. Rises can be rather hard so get ready–this is no time for 6X.

Black Caddis

This is the widespread small black caddis–the genus is *Chimarra*. The black caddis generally appears at the same time as the alder and is about a size 18 or 20. Often, especially if the river is down, the fish key in on the black caddis, to the exclusion of the much larger alder. This is due, in my opinion, to the fact that trout get very suspicious of large insects on hard-fished streams. The trout quickly learn that smaller is safer and key in on the micro patterns that are available such as the black caddis. This caddis can be imitated with a black dubbed body and a black deer or elk-hair wing with or without a black hackle wound at the front. The black caddis can be found on the water during most of the day but the trout will feed on the adults from late evening to dusk. Watch for sipping rises along the edge of faster flows as the sun starts to set. A quick check of the surface will usually reveal the hatching black caddis. If you get a refusal to an alder pattern try the black caddis dead-drifted over the fish's position and watch closely since the rises are very subtle.

Tan Caddis

The tan caddis hatches start appearing about the same time as the green caddis. There are numerous tan species on the river ranging from size 16 to 22. One species is about a size 16 and has tan wings and a brownish body. The tan caddis is one of the many caddis hatches that is available to the trout when they return to lay their eggs. The pocket picking technique described for the green caddis is effective here also. The key is to cover as much water as possible and to watch closely for trout rising to the egg-laying adults. Blind casting is usually counterproductive. When a riser is spotted, cover it as quickly as possible with a slack line cast. If that fails to induce a rise, try moving the imitation ever so slightly just as it get into the trout's window. The best time of day for this type of fishing is usually in the morning as the sun starts to warm up the river. I match the hatch with a hook to match the size of the adult, a dubbed body of the appropriate color and an elk-hair wing. In this way, I can match any of the river's numerous caddis hatches simply by capturing an adult and by following the above formula. I also carry some Henryville Specials or Green Caddis to give a tough fish a different look if it refuses the Elk Wing. During slow periods, or just before a hatch, fishing a Bead-head Caddis or a Caddis Worm on the bottom can be very effective. Good colors are olive, olive-brown and bright green. Soft hackles before and during a hatch can be deadly. My favorite soft hackle is the Partridge and Green.

Other Trout Food

Midges

Midge hatches become most important during the cold weather months. I have had good success during the months of November, March and April. During March and early April in particular, the shucks from the emerging midges can be so numerous that they form a one- or two-foot border along the edge of the stream. Look for low-water conditions and fish the Griffith's Gnat or a greased Mouse Turd fly in the film to sipping trout. The Mouse Turd fly is simply muskrat fur dubbed in a cigar shape on a size 20 hook. A friend that I had given some samples to returned with glowing reports and named the fly after what he thought they looked like—the name stuck, so to speak. Most of the Hous' midges are gray, black or olive and range in size from 20 to 28. One November afternoon I was fishing BWOs to visibly rising fish. After repeated rejections, I finally took a close look at the stream surface and noticed midges were on the menu and not the BWOs I had expected. A switch to the Mouse Turd fly brought instant acceptance from many large Hous browns. If you are fishing the river in the late fall or early spring, always be on the lookout for midges. Keep in mind, that midges are always available to the trout and they will feed on them even during the summer—especially in the early morning hours. A size 20 Griffith's Gnat will fool these early morning midge feeders before the main hatches begin.

Stoneflies

Stonefly nymphs are a major part of the diet of trout. Most stonefly nymphs are large (about 2 inches or more) and can be found primarily in the riffles. A large yellow or golden Stonefly Nymph fished in the pocket water is usually very productive. I have also had outstanding success with a size 10 Scraggly or size 10 Red Fox Squirrel Nymph both of which I believe are taken for stonefly nymphs. Since most of the nymphs crawl out and hatch on the boulders in the river usually at night, the emerging adults are not available to the trout. Also, I have not witnessed trout feeding on the surface to stoneflies, so dry-fly imitations are not needed.

Scuds

Every time I screen the bottom of the river, I am amazed at the number of scuds that show up. They range in color from gray to beige with tinges of olive. The Gold Ribbed Hare's Ear is a very effective fly on the river and one of the reasons, I believe, is that it is a good scud representation. I have tried many other scud imitations, but none are as effective as I think they should be considering the heavy concentrations of naturals. I have even tried some of the off-colors such as pink and orange with only fair success. The search for the killer scud pattern continues.

Crayfish and Hellgrammites

The river is simply loaded with crayfish. It's really tough to catch a trout on a crayfish imitation since the smallmouth bass love these critters. Cast a crayfish into a likely looking run and before it swings very far you will be fast to a smallie and it will probably have a crayfish already sticking out of its gullet. The Borger Fleeing Crayfish is one of my favorite imitations. Hellgrammites on the river are huge and obviously make a great meal for any fish. Black or olive Woolly Buggers are incredibly effective on the Housatonic and I believe it is because they are taken for crayfish and hellgrammites. Try coneheads or dumbbell eyes on Woolly Buggers; the jigging action causes the bass and trout to go crazy.

Terrestrials

In August and September flying ants can liven up the dry-fly fishing. It is really difficult to anticipate when the flying ants will show but if you are lucky enough to be there at the right time, the fishing can be exceptional. One flying ant is about a size 16 or 18 with a ginger color and the other I have witnessed is a size 24 in black. If you arrive at the river in the evening, during late summer, and the trout are sipping everywhere, suspect flying ants. Of course, you should check the surface to be sure. The regular ant pattern is effective all year especially in the smaller sizes. Another favorite terrestrial pattern is a green beetle in size 14. I don't know how many beetles are eaten by the trout but a black or green beetle has fooled many trout for me—especially when the trout were already up feeding on a hatch. Another favorite of mine is the Letort Cricket in size 12 or 14. I fish the cricket or beetle either as a hatch breaker or to drum up interest during non-hatch periods.

The late-fall menu includes midges and blue-winged olives.
Water levels and crowds can be the lowest of the year.

Chapter Four
FISHING NON-HATCH PERIODS

Let's face it, most of the time spent fly fishing is during non-hatch periods. In order to consistently score, a strategy is needed for those "bugless times." I usually count on nymphs, terrestrials or attractor dries in that order as the basis of my strategy.

Nymphs

I fish two nymphs 90 percent of the time when nymphing. I attach the first nymph to the tippet in the normal fashion. A second piece of tippet, about 12-18 inches long, is tied to the eye of the first nymph. You will now have two knots in the eye of the top nymph. Then simply tie the bottom nymph to the end of the second tippet piece. I attach the split shot, if needed, between the two nymphs. I have found that this way of rigging two flies tends to minimize tangles. Maintain an open loop during casting, and keep false casting to a minimum. If you allow the line to swing downstream after the drift, the rod will load from the water tension. Rotate your wrist to the rear casting position, then simply face upstream and move the rod forward in the normal casting motion. This little trick will eliminate the false casting that causes so many tangles with nymphs and split shot.

Good attractor nymphs are the Prince, Red Fox Squirrel Nymph, and Gold Ribbed Hare's Ear. All of these nymphs can be tied with or without beads although the beaded versions are usually more effective. I usually place the attractor nymph in the top position and a more representative type nymph in the lower position. (On New Mexico's San Juan River and other Western tailwaters, the top nymph is often a San Juan Worm and the bottom fly a midge larva or pupa imitation.) A good combination for the Housatonic at any time is the Prince Nymph on top with a caddis pupa imitation as the trailer. Many times the attractor nymph will cause the trout to investigate long enough to notice the smaller, more realistic nymph which it readily accepts.

Fishing two nymphs allows you to determine which is working much more quickly. If one fly is producing and the other is not, I change the least productive nymph until it too produces at least as well as the other. By doing this there is not much risk because you always have one fly on that you have confidence in and it allows you to experiment with flies that you may not ordinarily try. This can produce gratifying results and new "must haves" for the nymph box. In rare cases it may turn out that the best combination is two of the same nymph or the same nymph in different colors.

Good representative type nymphs are: Serendipities, Antron Caddis

Pupas, bead-head caddis worms, and fur mayfly and stonefly nymphs. Normally, I will fish only one bead-head fly at a time, since the bead-head's flash can turn the fish off, especially on bright days.

Terrestrials
For those blank days, when fishing blind with dry flies, I usually reach for a terrestrial first. When you consider the fact that a trout never knows when a terrestrial will fall into the river and the fact that many land insects are very much out of their element in the stream, it's no wonder trout respond to them with such gusto. Trout usually rise up for at least a look, allowing you to mark their position for a later attempt with something else.

Letort Crickets and foam beetles are two of the very best searching flies. They are also two of the very best hatch breakers–flies that work during a good hatch when the trout are just too selective. It's hard for a trout to resist the food value in just one plump cricket even in the middle of a flush hatch. Always carry ants on the Housatonic, they have saved the day for me more than once. I have had the best success with small ants sizes 18-22–they work particularly well during fall. I have fished brightly colored ants such as red or orange and the fish did not seem to mind the color at all and they are a lot easier to see. Fishing flying ant patterns in August and September in sizes 16 to 18 is usually productive even when there are not any naturals on the water–the trout expect to see them.

Attractor Dries
Attractor dry flies are underused and underappreciated. That's a shame because attractors can coax up wily browns and rainbows when nothing else will, if you know when and how to fish them. Size 12 and 14 flies can be very effective if the river is up–say above 400 cfs. Humpies, White Wulffs, Ausable Wulffs, Parachute Adams, and Trudes all work. My favorite is a Parachute Adams with a gold poly wing and a tan body in a size 14 called a EMBT on the Beaverkill River. The gold wing shows up well, both for the angler and the trout. One beautiful June evening, fishing the pocket water above the covered bridge, I landed over 20 fish on that fly during a two-hour span. Fish attractor dries in the pocket water between the pools when the river is up slightly, you'll be pleasantly surprised with the results.

Cows feeding along a bucolic stretch of the Housatonic.

Chapter Five
SMALLMOUTH BASS FISHING

It's a misty July morning and I'm working my way up the river in relative solitude. Then I see them–two guys trout fishing. They are fishing with flies so small they can't see them and with 7X and 8X tippets with their 2-weight rods, they think they have a chance. They don't. The trout are not there. A month earlier, this spot and others like them were very productive but the trout have since moved off to the mouth of tributaries because of the elevated water temperatures. As I get out of the stream to pass them, they call over.

"You seem to be doing well, what are you using?"

"Dahlberg Divers," I reply, "I'm bass fishing."

"Oh, bass," is the usual reply and I smile as I move on to catch more hard-fighting smallmouths while they continue to try to outwit a few wily dace.

This scene is repeated many times during the course of a Housy summer. Smallmouth bass don't get any respect from most fly-fishers. Trout get the lion's share of the attention and when the trout fishing slows during the summer, the river can be almost deserted. Don't make that mistake.

Smallmouth fishing seems to come on as the trout fishing slows down. As the water temperatures approach 70 degrees, the bass' metabolism goes into high gear and they become eating machines. The bass are not fussy either, they will take surface poppers, dries, streamers, wets, and nymphs. The warmer the water, the more likely the bass will strike. It is not unusual to catch two to three dozen bass in an evening of fishing on the Hous if you are fishing for them.

Water levels have settled down by June most years and the releases are usually very dependable, with low water in the morning and evening. Wading can be done wet with a pair of sneakers and with the addition of a fly box and nippers and tippet material, you are ready for action.

The bass are great fighters and will usually jump when hooked. Smallmouths as large as 19 inches have been reported from reliable sources, but the average size is about a pound. However, on a typical day, you will catch a few bass over 12 inches and bass of that size will give you quite a fight.

The most successful bass anglers target the bass specifically. Bass in most cases require different tackle, techniques, and flies than trout. A few Hous regulars will carry two rods for a day on the river especially in the fall, one for bass and one for trout. Keep in mind that elevated water temperatures (above 75 degrees) during the summer will cause the trout to pool up in thermal refuges which are typically the mouths of feeders and some spring holes. It is illegal to fish within 100 feet of the feeders from June 15th to September 1st. Catching a trout under high water-temperature times is almost always fatal to the trout. Even with water temperatures above 70 degrees the trout can become stressed and they certainly don't fight very well under those circumstances. However, during these high water-temperature conditions, the silver lining is that the main stem of the river will be practically empty of trout but loaded with hungry bass. They have the main river virtually to themselves and seem to know it. The message therefore, is simple, fish for the bass with bass-type flies and leave the trout alone during warm-water periods. So let us look at bass tactics a little more closely.

Tackle

An 8- to 9-foot rod for 7- or 8-weight line is perfect for river smallmouths. The flies can be bulky and less than aerodynamic so the 7- or 8-weight line will handle these flies very well. I prefer to use weight-forward floating lines for all my bass work on the Housatonic. The bass tapers can be useful in turning a fly over in a breeze but they do not cast as smoothly as the regular weight-forwards. Sink-tip lines or lead-core leaders can be helpful if you like them, especially when the river is high. Reels need not be fancy, I have been using a Pfleuger for many years. A dependable single action reel is all that is needed.

Leaders must be strong. A 7 1/2-foot leader tapered to 1X will handle the requirements of these tough fish. Smallmouths have a habit of diving to the bottom of the river and running the leader over the numerous rocks that carpet the Hous. Check your leader for nicks often and replace as necessary. The saltwater leaders and tippet material with their superior abrasion resistance are an excellent choice on the Housatonic. The increased diameter of these materials also helps in turning over the flies. Smallmouths are not leader shy especially on the sunken offerings. A common mistake is to use trout leaders for bass fishing which usually leads to casting difficulties and lost fish and flies. Trout gear works well when the bass are rising to dry flies, the best example being the white fly hatch in early August. During the white fly hatch, a 3- or 4-weight rod and a size 14 White Wulff can provide a great evening of fun.

Location

Bass-feeding lies are generally different than trout-feeding lies. Usually, bass prefer slower water than trout and will venture into very shallow water to feed. For instance, bass move into water barely covering their backs along the river's edge looking for crayfish, especially during low-light periods.

To illustrate the difference between trout and bass lies, imagine a large boulder in the middle of the flow. Trout may be found directly in front of the rock in the cushion or along the edges of the flow as it passes the boulder on each side. And the bass? Most likely in the dead water directly behind the boulder. Needless to say, getting a good drift through that area is not exactly easy, but then again, in most cases, it is not needed–more on that later.

Even though bass do venture into shallow areas to feed, they prefer deep, slow holes and pockets. If you can locate a deep hole in an otherwise shallow run, that hole will hold an amazing number of bass and undoubtedly some monsters. When the river is down, use this opportunity to identify those holes and pockets and it will pay off later. When the river is very low during the heat of the summer, most of the bass will be in those holes and pockets–fish them very carefully.

As stated earlier, bass have a fondness for boulders, especially large ones with dead water behind them. Bass can also be found near rock ledges that drop off into deeper water. And like most fish, bass like shade. The shadier side of a rock is always worth that first cast and the shadier side of the river is usually more productive.

Flies

Surface

A smallmouth smashing a surface fly is always exciting. Many times bass will take a fly the instant it hits the water causing the most uncoordinated responses by the angler but it always adds up to a lot of fun.

The Dahlberg Diver is my favorite surface fly for river bass. Well greased up, the fly will dive when retrieved and float back to the surface as tension is released. Tails on the Dahlberg can be made of saddle hackles, rabbit strips or marabou. The tail material should move in the currents when the fly is at rest. Yellow and chartreuse are very effective colors and are easy to track.

Lefty Kreh, many years ago, designed a cork fly called the Lefty's Bug for the smallmouths on the Potomac River. It has a short tail of squirrel and a short semicircle body with no appendages coming off it in order to make the fly cast well and not foul. The Lefty's Bug should be in your fly box. Another effective "bug" is the Sneaky Pete. The Sneaky Pete is similar to Lefty's Bug but has long rubber legs that move enticingly and a cone-shaped face.

Terrestrials, such as beetles and crickets, are always effective. A hopper pattern or Muddler Minnow can be fished dry and retrieved wet–a very deadly technique. When the flying ants make their appearance in late summer, a size 14 flying ant pattern will bring the bass up all day long.

Match-the-hatch dry-fly action can also be had with bass. The best hatches for bass tend to be those of the summer and fall. Bass like their flies on the large side. Alders, cahills, the white fly, and *Isonychia* are all bass favorites. The white fly is head and shoulders above the rest though as the premier hatch in bringing the big bass up to the top. The bass work themselves into a frenzy as the white flies hatch, mate and fall to the surface in a short period of time starting at dusk and lasting until well after dark. The hatch can be so thick that indeed it looks like a blizzard in August. The White Wulff and a simple white spinner are the two most effective patterns.

Subsurface

Without a doubt, the number one subsurface fly in popularity is the Woolly Bugger. Tied with an olive body and a black marabou tail, the Bugger looks a little like everything. The Hous is loaded with hellgrammites and crayfish which can be represented very well by the Woolly Bugger. Dead-drift presentations upstream can be especially effective. Buggers with different color combinations and/or lead dumbbell eyes can also deadly.

My favorite subsurface flies are crayfish patterns. Borger's Fleeing Crayfish is a relatively simple tie with most of its movement coming from a rabbit strip on the hook bend. The fly represents a crayfish leaving the scene. The dumbbell eyes get the fly to the bottom which is key. (I have seen smallmouths pin the fly to the bottom much the way they attack the natural.) The eyes on top of the hook shank cause the fly to flip over so the hook point is up, allowing the angler to snake the fly over the bottom relatively snag-free. Casting the fly so that it sinks into the deep holes followed by a slow hopping retrieve will almost always bring a violent strike. Another good crayfish pattern is the Fuzzabunny, which has a rabbit strip tail, dumbbell eyes, and a body of sheep's wool or a wound rabbit strip. Olive is the standard color for the Fuzzabunny.

Most streamer patterns work very well, the Muddler Minnow and the Matuka are two of the best. The Clouser Minnow was invented by Bob Clouser for smallmouths and is used today to catch just about every game fish–fresh and salt. It's still a heck of a smallmouth fly. I like the chartreuse over white, and the tan over white versions. In addition, don't forget wet flies, if you carry only one, make it the Alder Fly. Peacock herl has a special magic on the Hous and many smallmouths have fallen for the venerable Alder.

The Prince Nymph is probably the number one nymph pattern for bass and trout (peacock herl again). Stonefly nymphs–especially the Montana Stone, Hare's Ear and Whitlock's Red Fox Squirrel nymph–have all produced big for me at one time or another.

There is one oddball fly that seems to produce when all else fails. It's actually an epoxy bonefish fly with a marabou tail. Tied on a size 6 hook, this fly works so well that I now tie them specifically for bass. The olive or brown colors seem to work the best. The fly casts like a dream and attracts those selective bass for some reason–probably because they don't get to see many bonefish flies.

Tactics

Bass require the same care in approach as trout. Loud wading and careless casting will send bass scurrying just as quickly as trout. However, there are some differences in tactics for bass that are worth noting.

When casting dry flies or surface bugs such as the Dahlberg, drag can work for you. Many times a fly struggling on the surface attracts bass when a dead-drift presentation will be ignored. I have cast a White Wulff, for instance, in the midst of hundreds of mayflies and gotten a take immediately upon twitching the fly. This is why, when casting behind boulders, it is not as big a presentation problem as it appears. The fly will float for a few seconds dead drift (and usually be ignored) and then as the current catches the fly line, the fly will start to drag and the bass' predator streak takes over and it slams the fly before it can escape.

Allowing the dry fly to sink below the surface is another tactic that can be incredibly effective. I discovered this one day when my much saturated fly would occasionally sink below the surface and be immediately taken by a bass. Floating high and dry, with or without drag, the fly was ignored time and again. Finally the light went on and I deliberately allowed the fly to sink on every cast. Bingo!, fish after fish. Since that time long ago, I have always used the sinking fly technique when the dry-fly fishing gets tough, with great results. Watch the area where the fly is for a swirl or flash that indicates the take. Most of the time, however, the bass will take with such authority that they will hook themselves.

When casting surface bugs like Dahlbergs and Lefty's Bug, the key is to try different retrieves. Let it sit, retrieve fast or slow—experiment until the bass tell you what they want that day. My standard cast is quartering up- or downstream and I let the current move the fly. Many times, just the waking action of the bug is enough to elicit a strike. As the fly approaches a boulder or other obstruction I speed up the retrieve and then slow it down, which many times results in a strike. Cast above good holding water and work the fly down into the hot area. Remember to keep your rod tip down and pointed at the fly in order to maintain good contact with the fly. Move the fly by retrieving with your line hand, not by moving the rod, moving the rod will cause slack. By eliminating the slack in the line, you will be able to set the hook much more effectively.

When fishing weighted flies such as those with dumbbell eyes, I like to let the fly sink to the bottom and remain motionless for a few seconds. Many times a bass will hit the fly on the drop, so be prepared. I then retrieve the fly slowly, over the bottom, maintaining contact with the fly at all times in order to feel the pickup from the bass. If possible, keep the fly in sight—don't forget those Polaroids! A fly with some white in it, like a Clouser, can help out a lot here. If you can see the fly and it disappears, chances are a bass has it in its mouth—tighten up and if you feel the fish, set the hook with a slipstrike. Bass can be very quick at picking up a fly and dropping it so you must pay strict attention. Change to an all-white fly if you are missing too many takes.

Bass tend to be most active during the summer and fall. As water temperatures drop in fall, surface activity will become less important and subsurface feeding more important. In October, bass, like trout, tend to feed with more abandon, as if they know that winter is approaching. The fishing will remain good until water temperatures drop below 50 degrees. October is a good time of year to spend the morning fishing for bass and the afternoon casting for trout during the olive hatches. I always bring a bass rod and a trout rod in the fall—sort of a Hous blast-and-cast, the smallmouths being the blast.

Major Mayfly Hatches

GENUS	SPECIES	FREQUENCY	EARLY DATE	LATE DATE	COMMON NAME	DUN TIME	SPINNER TIME
Baetis	species	C	April	October	Blue-winged Olive	M, A*	A
Ephemerella	subvaria	A	April 15	May 15	Hendrickson	M, A*	E**
Stenonema	vicarium	C	May 20	June 15	March Brown	A	E
Stenonema	fuscum	C	May 15	June 10	Gray Fox	A	E
Ephemera	simulans	A	May 20	June 10	Brown Drake	E	E, X
Ephemerella	dorothea	A	May 25	June 30	Sulphur	E*	E
Ephemera	guttulata	I	May 20	June 15	Green Drake	A, E	E, X
Ephemerella	cornutella	I	May 20	June 30	Blue-winged Olive	E	E
Serratella	deficiens	A	May 20	June 30	Blue-winged Olive	M	E
Stenonema	ithaca	C	June 1	Aug. 30	Light Cahill	A, E	E
Stenacron	canadense	C	June 1	Aug. 30	Light Cahill	A, E	E
Tricorythodes	species	I	July 1	Sept. 30	Trico	M	M
Ephoron	leukon	A	Aug. 1	Aug. 30	White Fly	E	E, X
Isonychia	bicolor	C	July 15	Sept. 30	Dun Variant	A, E	E
Isonychia	sadleri	C	Sept. 1	Oct. 30	Dun Variant	A, E	E

FOOTNOTES

Frequency: A = abundant, C = common, I = infrequent

Early Date/Late Date: Dates provided are the average dates during which maximum hatching might be expected to occur. These dates assume normal climatic conditions.

Common Names: Various common names might be found for each species, and often the same common name is applied to different species. Thus we have provided the proper mayfly name to avoid confusion.

Hatching Times: The hatch times given are for normal climatic conditions. Spinner falls, in particular, are very temperature dependent.

M = morning, N = noon, A = afternoon, E = evening, X = night, * = super hatch, ** = super spinner fall

Other Hatches

Common Name	Early Date	Late Date	Size
Green Caddis	May 1	June 30	16-18
Tan Caddis	May 1	July 15	16-20
Alder	June 1	August 1	12
Black Caddis	June 1	September 15	18-20
Terrestrials			
Flying Ants	July 15	October 31	14-24
Midges *Diptera*	All year	All year	20-28

Strategy session.

Pine Swamp Brook waterfall before it enters the Housatonic.

Fishing the head of Garbage Hole. This pool received its name from a large eddy that forms during high water, collecting much river debris during storms.

JOHN BELLOWS

Trout Flies

Floating Pheasant Tail Nymph

Hook: TMC 900BL, #20-24.
Body: Pheasant tail.
Tail: Pheasant tail.
Wingcase: Gray poly.

During BWO hatches trout will often feed on emergers. This fly was designed to represent that stage. I knew that a sunken Pheasant Tail Nymph was effective during BWO hatches and so, to make the emerger, I simply added poly to the top of the fly. It has been lethal during BWO emergences. It can also be fished with micro-shot and indicator when the trout are taking the nymphs below the surface.

Use about three pheasant tail fibers and tie them in at the rear of the hook so that the tips will form the tail. Wind the pheasant tail fibers forward to the eye and tie off. Reinforce the body by winding thread to the rear and forward again. Dub the thread with the gray poly and raise the thread above the hook at the wingcase position. Push the dubbing down and thread to the hook shank to form a ball. Wind in front and back of the ball to secure. Form the head and whip-finish.

Rabbit Foot Emerger

Hook: TMC 2487, #12-18.
Body: Synthetic or dyed fur.
Tail: Brown Z-lon.
Wing: Snowshoe rabbit foot.
Throat: CDC.

I first saw this fly described in an article by Tom Rosenbauer of Orvis. I don't know if this is Tom's invention but it sure is a winner. It is especially effective during Hendrickson hatches.

Tie in a short tail of brown Z-lon. Dub the body with the appropriate color for the emerger. (For Hendricksons, I use a dark rusty-brown.) Attach the wing so that it slopes back over the body short of the tail. Apply a throat of CDC fibers and tie off the head. The thread wrappings can be covered with a rough dubbing such as hare's ear. Imagine incorporating CDC, hare's ear and snowshoe rabbit foot into one fly–the trout don't stand a chance.

Mouse Turd Fly

Hook: TMC 900BL, #20, TMC 101, #22.
Thread: Black.
Body: Muskrat underfur.

You want simplicity, here it is. Dub the muskrat underfur onto the hook forming a rough cigar shape. That's it. If some of the guard hairs end up in the dubbing, that's OK too.

Fish this fly in the surface film to represent midge pupae. Don't laugh, this fly has taken an amazing number of fish both in the East and West. It is particularly effective on selective fish that are eating minutia in the film. There's a certain weird satisfaction in taking those tough eaters on this fly.

The fly received its name from Bill Goeben, a Hous veteran, who, when I gave it to him, thought it looked like . . . well, a mouse turd. Can you imagine?

Emerger

Hook: TMC 900BL, #16-20.
Thread: Brown or olive.
Body: Dark brown camel hair.
Tail: None.
Wing: Snowshoe rabbit foot colored with yellow/gold Pantone pen (#137).

Use the Pantone pen to color a portion of the snowshoe rabbit foot. Work the color into the fur, all the way to the skin. When dry, cut off a piece of the rabbit foot for a wing, cutting from the skin level. Cut enough material to give yourself good floatation, the fly floats on its wing. Tie in the rabbit foot material with the tips pointing over the eyes and tie down at the wing position with about five wraps. Clip off the butt end as close as possible and wind the thread to the rear to secure the material to the hook. Raise the wing with many wraps in front of the wing, in the manner of a Compara-dun. Dub the body with the camel hair, making sure to apply some directly in front of the wing, tie off and you are done.

I usually don't grease this fly at all. It fishes down in the film and looks very vulnerable to the trout. This fly works well as a sulphur emerger in size 16 or 18. It also works well in size 20 for the larger *Baetis* hatches. Also, this emerger has been the most effective fly, by far, for PMD hatches I have fished on Montana's Madison and Missouri rivers.

Griffith's Gnat

Hook: TMC 501, #20-24,
TMC 101, #20-24.
Thread: Black.
Body: Peacock herl.
Hackle: Grizzly.

This is a must-have fly for those times the trout are sipping some mystery item from the surface. If you find a trout rising early in the morning, before the major hatches of the day start, chances are it is feeding on midges and the Griffith's Gnat will be readily accepted. Size 22 is the size I use most often, tied on the TMC 101 hook.

I discovered another variation of this fly in Ross Mueller's remarkable book, *Upper Midwest Flies That Catch Trout.* Simply tie in a grizzly hackle at the rear of the hook and Super Glue the shank. Wind the hackle forward and tie off. This version works particularly well in the smaller sizes.

Elk Wing Caddis

Hook: TMC 900BL, #14-20.
Thread: To match the body.
Abdomen: Synthetic dubbing or dyed fur.
Wing: Elk hair or deer hair.

This is my standard caddis pattern. For the green caddis, I use a size 16 hook and a grayish-olive dubbing with the standard light elk-hair wing. For the black caddis, black deer hair and black dubbing are used on a size 20 hook. You get the idea. I find that the body of the caddis in the surface film is usually much more effective for selective fish than the high floaters such as the standard Elk Hair Caddis with its palmered body. If a trout refuses this fly, I switch to a hackled pattern with feathered wings such as the Henryville Special in the appropriate size. That usually does the trick.

Gold Poly-Wing Parachute (EMBT)

Hook: TMC 900BL, #14.
Thread: Tan.
Body: Fly-Rite #20, dark tan.
Wing: Gold poly.
Hackle: Grizzly dyed firey red-brown–tied parachute style.
Tail: Grizzly dyed firey red-brown.

This fly was first shown to me one June day on the banks of the Beaverkill River (where it is known as the EMBT–Ed McQuat's Brown Thing) by Bob Johnson. On the return trip home, I stopped at the Hous and tried the fly out. The browns and rainbows jumped all over it. Not only was the fly effective, but the gold wing made tracking the fly very easy. That evening occurred many years ago, but the EMBT has continued to produce year in and year out. It is much like the Adams, a fly that does not represent anything exactly, but looks a little like a lot of insects. It has been particularly successful in June when it is probably taken for an alder and during the fall when it most likely represents the *Isonychia*. Whatever the trout think it is, they sure do eat it, especially in the pocket water when the river is up a bit.

The dyed grizzly hackles can be obtained from Al Briganti of Al's Grizzly Farm in Belchertown, Mass. Al dyes necks specifically for Beaverkill regulars looking for the proper shade to tie the EMBT. A fiery red-brown neck can be used as a substitute.

Wingless Sulphur

Hook: TMC 900BL, #16-18.
Thread: Pale yellow.
Body: Abdomen–cream fur; Thorax–pale orange fur.
Tail: Cream hackle fibers.
Hackle: Cream hackle fibers wound over thorax.

This Ed Shenk pattern has been a consistent winner for me during sulphur hatches. Ed is from Carlisle, Pennsylvania where they take their sulphur hatches and patterns very seriously. (By the way, Ed is also the inventor of the Letort Cricket, another dynamite fly.) The Sulphur can be tied with one hackle if you use a domestic cape, otherwise use two stiff hackles.

Sparkle Dun

Hook: TMC 900BL.
Thread: To match body color.
Body: Synthetic or dyed fur.
Tail: Z-lon.
Wing: Deer hair.

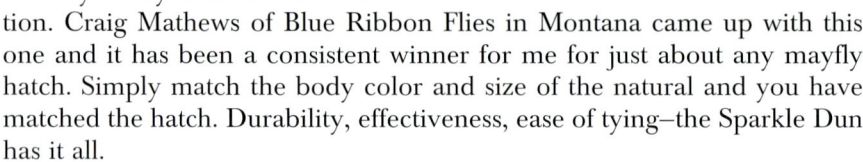

This fly is my standard dun imitation. Craig Mathews of Blue Ribbon Flies in Montana came up with this one and it has been a consistent winner for me for just about any mayfly hatch. Simply match the body color and size of the natural and you have matched the hatch. Durability, effectiveness, ease of tying–the Sparkle Dun has it all.

First, tie in a small bunch of stacked deer hair so that the tips project over the eye of the hook. The wing should be the length of the body. Secure the deer hair and trim off the butt ends as close as possible. Wind the thread back to the rear of the fly to anchor the wing to the hook shank. Tie in the tail of Z-lon which represents the nymph shuck. And, as a general rule, I use brown but I don't think the color really matters. Raise the wing and put numerous wraps in front of the wing to keep the wing straight up or tilted slightly to the rear. Dub the body taking care to put some of the dubbing right in front of the wing.

Brown Drake Parachute

Hook: Mustad 94831, #8-10.
Thread: Brown.
Body: Brown fur or synthetic dubbing.
Tail: Grizzly hackle
Wing: Deer hair post
Hackle. Grizzly.

When you need a good brown drake imitation you really need a good brown drake imitation. The trout feed with apparent abandon but will actually be quite selective as to size and shape. The madness never lasts for long so it pays to always carry a few Brown Drake Parachutes in early June. This imitation has proven itself over the years and has the added benefit of being a good floater. This basic design can be modified for use for any large mayfly such as the green drake or March brown simply by using the appropriate hook size and body color.

The Route 4/7 bridge is the bottom boundary of the TMA. Good fishing exists for several miles below the bridge.

BWO Parachute

Hook: TMC 501, #20-24, TMC 101, #20-24.
Thread: Olive.
Abdomen: Olive thread.
Thorax: Olive dubbing.
Tail: Ginger hackle fibers.
Wing: White or gray poly or Hi-Vis fibers.
Hackle: Blue dun or ginger.

In the fall, this is the standard BWO pattern fished on the river. Some people tie this fly down to a size 28 but I limit the insanity to a size 24. The parachute hackle is optional, and I have found that the fly usually fishes just as well without the hackle. (Also, it is much easier to tie.) I use the white wing more often than the gray since the white is much easier to spot on a choppy surface and the trout don't seem to mind the white wing.

Henryville Special

Hook: TMC 900BL, #14-20.
Thread: Olive.
Body: Green floss palmered with a grizzly hackle.
Underwing: Wood duck breast feather barbules.
Overwing: Mallard wing feathers.
Hackle: Brown.

This classic Eastern caddis pattern is still a winner after all these years. A size 18 Henryville Special fished in the pocket water is deadly. Don't leave home without this one.

King River Caddis

- **Hook:** Mustad 94840, #12.
- **Thread:** Black.
- **Body:** Orange floss or peacock herl.
- **Rib:** Grizzly or brown hackle-trimmed short.
- **Wing:** Well-marked turkey.
- **Hackle:** Brown.

The first year I went to Montana I tied some of these. I never used them. They rattled around in my fly box for a couple of years until I noticed that the wings were a very good match to the alders on the Hous. The trout agreed.

I continue to tie this pattern with the orange floss body because it works, but in many cases I will substitute peacock herl for the floss since peacock is a much better match for the body color of the natural. I trim the palmered grizzly hackle to hook gap length or less. The key to this fly is the wings; they should be well-mottled turkey, reinforced with vinyl cement or even rubber cement. Golden pheasant tail feathers have excellent markings for the alder but they are very fragile.

Spent Partridge Caddis

- **Hook:** TMC 900BL, #14-18.
- **Thread:** Brown or olive.
- **Body:** Olive fur or synthetic dubbing.
- **Thorax:** Peacock herl.
- **Wing:** Partridge feather.
- **Hackle:** Brown and grizzly.

A Mike Lawson pattern designed for the tough rainbows of the Henry's Fork in Idaho but equally effective on the Housatonic. When the caddis return, mate and eventually die, many of the adults will be found in the surface film and the trout, recognizing an easy meal, will dine on these delicate morsels with a gentle sip, especially at sunset.

Dub the rear 2/3 of the hook and attach a partridge feather so that it lays flat over the back of the fly and extends a short distance past the body. The thorax will have peacock herl with a brown and grizzly hackle wound through the peacock and tied off at the head. Trim the hackle flat on the top and bottom.

Green Caddis

Hook: TMC 900BL, #16-18.
Thread: Brown or olive.
Body: Olive dubbing.
Rib: Grizzly hackle.
Wing: Turkey feather or synthetic wing material.
Hackle: Brown.

Good caddis patterns are crucial for consistent fishing success on the Housatonic. One of the best is this green caddis imitation which can be altered in size and color to match any of the numerous caddis hatches on the river. The grizzly hackle rib is palmered up the body and should not be longer than the hook gap. The wing material can be turkey quill that has been reinforced with rubber glue or synthetic wing materials. By the way, Swiss straw, when unfolded, makes a very effective wing material.

Partridge and Green

Hook: TMC 9300, #12-18.
Body: Green thread or floss.
Thorax: Small ball of hare's ear.
Wing: One or two wraps of partridge feather.

I use Pearsal's Silk to tie this fly but it is not necessary—it's the traditional tying thread for the soft hackles or "spiders" of the English Isles. The small ball of dubbing behind the hackles holds the hackles up a bit and allows the fly to "swim" in a lifelike manner. Another surprisingly effective combination is the Starling and Purple tied on a size 16 or 18 hook or try the March Brown Spider which has a body of hare's ear ribbed with gold wire and a partridge wing.

The way I most enjoy fishing soft hackles is to cast them upstream to active or rising fish. The fly will sink just a few inches below the surface and the trout will take it usually with a swirl. It takes a bit more concentration to follow the fly, and to observe it, but the reward of the take is well worth it. If you haven't tried soft hackles, especially fished in this manner, give it a try and I think you'll discover they are lethal but most importantly, fun to fish.

Foam Beetle

Hook: TMC 900BL, #14.
Thread: Olive.
Body: Peacock herl.
Overbody: Foam––various colors.
Legs: Black Krystal Flash.

I believe the reason most people don't fish beetles more often is that they are usually tied in black, and black flies in the film are hard to see. Even beetles tied with yarn as an indicator are difficult to follow. I have experimented with different colored foam–red, green, blue, orange and white– and I have found that trout, in most cases, don't care what color your beetle is wearing. So if the trout don't particularly care, I'm going to use colors that are easy for me to see on the water. (My favorites colors are green and orange.) White is the most visible and the bottom of any beetle can be colored a most respectable black with a permanent marker.

Tie a foam strip in at the rear of the hook winding slightly down the bend of the hook. Tie in a couple of strands of peacock herl and then Super Glue the shank. Wind the peacock forward and tie off at the head. Pull the foam strip forward and tie off a couple of eye lengths behind the eye. Trim the foam over the eye to look like a head and attach three or four strands of Krystal Flash at the tie-down point and trim to size. The beetle can be tied in any size although I usually use size 14, and occasionally size 22, tied without the peacock herl.

CDC Ant

Hook: TMC 900BL, #14-22.
Thread: Brown.
Body: Ginger beaver fur or synthetic dubbing.
Legs: Pearl or black Krystal Flash–three or four strands.
Wing: White CDC.

Dub the rear portion of the ant starting slightly down the bend of the hook and ending about 1/3 of the way up the shank. Leave a space and attach the Krystal Flash with figure-eight wraps in the open area and then proceed to dub the forward section which should be much smaller than the rear section. Using the tip section of a CDC feather, attach the fibers in front of the first section so that they rise up over the body. Whip-finish and trim the Krystal Flash legs to size.

The CDC feather makes this fly very easy to see which is particularly important in the smaller sizes. (I usually eliminate the legs in the smallest sizes.) Ant patterns are a must-have item from late summer through the fall.

Serendipity

Hook: TMC 9300, #14-18,
Dai Riki 135, #14-18.
Thread: Red or to match the body color.
Body: Olive, red or brown Z-lon.
Ribbing: Gold wire.
Wing: Deer hair or elk hair.

I tie this fly the old-fashioned way, the way its creator Ross Marigold showed me many years ago. Today the commercial versions of this pattern twist the Z-lon body material to form the body segmentation but the original version used gold wire to get that effect. I also think that the gold wire adds a bit of sparkle that adds to the appeal. The Z-lon and gold wire are attached slightly past the hook bend. The Z-lon is wrapped up to the eye and tied off. Next, the gold wire is wound up to the eye and tied off. A small bunch of deer or elk hair is tied in at the eye, on top of the hook, with the tips extending back toward the bend of the hook. Don't worry about the length of the deer hair because it will be cut off later. Secure the deer hair and create a prominent head with the thread about twice the length of a normal head and whip-finish. Cut the deer hair off about 1/3 to 1/2 of the way back on the body of the fly forming a wingcase. I usually use red thread to tie Serendipities because that is the way Ross always tied them but I have found that the fly fishes equally well when the thread color matches the body. Of course, the Serendipity can be tied with a bead head.

It's hard to tell what this fly represents but it's another one that surely produces. All of the colors work, but I have found that on the Hous, the red version is the most effective for some reason. Perhaps it represents a midge worm. The brown and olive versions most likely represent caddis pupae. The Serendipity was invented in Montana on the Madison River, but it works anywhere there are caddis and midge hatches.

Lloyd Banquer shows off a 16-inch brown trout.

RS-2

Hook: TMC 900BL, #18-22.
Thread: Black.
Body: Gray muskrat or beaver.
Wingcase: Clump of down from the base of a pheasant feather—cut off halfway down the shank.
Tails: Micro Fibetts, split.

This fly is very effective during the fall BWO hatches. Rim Chung from Colorado invented this pattern to imitate the *Baetis* nymphs and it is especially deadly wherever these nymphs are found. I fish it just under the surface with a microshot and indicator during the hatch. The RS-2 is also effective when fished as a trailer in a two-nymph rig with a bead head as the top fly.

Scraggly

Hook: Mustad 9672, #6-18.
Thread: Black.
Body: Peacock herl with palmered, clipped grizzly hackle.
Hackle: Hen furnace hackle—on one side barbules are trimmed down to 3/16 inch.

This pattern is the creation of Connecticut's own Russ Ryder, master fly tier and peacock herl guru. As mentioned before, peacock herl flies are very effective on the Housatonic and this is one of the best. I like to fish this fly in the larger sizes in late summer and fall when the *Isonychia* nymphs are active. In smaller sizes, the Scraggly is a good caddis pupa imitation.

Bead-head Caddis

Hook: Dai Riki 135, #12-18, Nymph hook, #12-18.
Head: Brass or silver bead.
Thread: Olive.
Body: Olive-brown dubbing.
Rib: Gold wire.

The Housatonic is primarily a caddis river and the Bead-head Caddis is a deadly caddis pupa imitation. Fish these dead-drift and also try a retrieve, sometimes the extra movement draws vicious strikes. The Partridge SLF dubbing #11 is one of my favorite dubbings for this fly. Antron dubbings are also very effective. A turn or two of a soft hackle behind the bead head is optional. If extra weight is needed, try the Orvis tungston beads which are about 50 percent heavier than the equivalent-sized brass beads. Quite often, by using the tungston beads, the need for split shot is eliminated—always a happy prospect.

Bead-head Prince

Hook: Nymph hook, #12-16.
Thread: Red.
Body: Peacock herl.
Rib: Gold wire.
Tail: Brown goose biots.
Wingcase: White goose biots.
Hackle: Brown.

If you only fish one nymph on the Hous, this should be it. The Bead-head Prince and the regular Prince have probably caught more fish in recent years than any other single nymph. I use red thread on my Prince Nymphs–it's the Ross Marigold influence again, that's the way he tied them. I also like the way the fly looks with a red head. (By the way, Ross used red thread on all of his nymphs because he was color blind, it looked brown to him.)

Red Fox Squirrel Nymph (RFSN)

Hook: Mustad 3906B, #6-16.
Thread: Orange.
Tail: Red fox squirrel back fur.
Abdomen: Red fox squirrel belly fur mixed with Antron.
Rib: Gold wire.
Thorax: Red fox squirrel back fur mixed with Antron.

This is the famous Dave Whitlock pattern and I believe it is effective on the Hous because its unusual color scheme presents a different "look" than the typical artificial nymph. The bigger sizes are used during the colder months to catch large trout and bass. It is most likely taken then for a stonefly nymph. Whatever the reason, this fly works all year long. A turn or two of partridge at the head in a size 16 or 14 makes a good caddis pupa imitation. A bead can be added to the head, of course.

Bass Flies

Fuzzabunny

- **Hook:** Mustad 3366, #2.
- **Thread:** Olive.
- **Tail:** Rabbit strip.
- **Body:** Wound rabbit strip or sheep fleece dubbed and trimmed.
- **Eyes:** Dumbbell eyes, 1/36 oz.

Secure the eyes behind the eye of the hook and on top of the shank. Attach the tail making it about twice as long as the body. Attach another rabbit strip and wind it up to the eye of the hook, figure-eighting the eyes. If you prefer, sheep fleece body can be dubbed on and trimmed to shape. Olive has been the most productive color with rusty brown being a good second choice.

Greg Smith first showed me this fly with the sheep fleece body. The rabbit-strip body is much easier to tie and seems to be as effective. The fly that Greg gave me caught over 100 bass over many seasons until a large fish finally broke me off. Needless to say, I have been tying my own ever since.

Dahlberg Diver

- **Hook:** Mustad 3366, #2.
- **Thread:** To match body.
- **Tail:** Rabbit strip, marabou or saddle hackle.
- **Body and Head:** Deer hair trimmed to shape.

This fly is not easy to tie at first but like everything else, with a little practice they are not that difficult. The deer hair is spun and trimmed into the diver shape which allows the fly to dive when retrieved and float back to the surface when the tension is released. Effective colors are olive, yellow, white and the natural brown. This is my most effective surface fly for bass and the most fun to fish. The bass hit this bug with such ferocity that it never fails to amaze me.

Fleeing Crayfish

- **Hook:** Mustad 9671, #4-10.
- **Thread:** Rusty brown.
- **Tail:** Olive-green marabou—as long as the shank.
- **Body:** Rusty brown fur.
- **Eyes:** Chrome-plated lead eyes tied on top of the hook shank.
- **Hackle:** Iridescent bronze body feather from pheasant with marabou fluff.
- **Fur Strip:** Rusty brown.

This fly is a Gary Borger pattern from his incredible book, *Designing Trout Flies*. The fur strip is attached to the hook by pulling the fur-strip end over the hook point. The fly will ride upside-down because of the lead eyes, therefore the strip should attached so that the fur side of the strip will ride up when the fly is retrieved. See Gary's book for complete instructions.

I like to cast this fly into likely holes and let it drop to the bottom. Watch carefully, the bass will often take this fly on the drop or while it is motionless on the bottom. Of course, with all the soft materials, this fly is never really motionless. I then move it slowly over the bottom, constantly maintaining contact with the fly. The bass will quite often pin this fly to the bottom which makes me believe that they are taking it for a crayfish.

Crayfish this big appeal to raccoons more than bass.

Treat yourself
and your angling partner . . .

...to a fly fishing and tying feast with subscriptions to **Flyfishing & Tying Journal.** You'll marvel at the helpful, colorful creativity inside this 100-plus page quarterly masterpiece of publishing!

You've worked hard, now sit back and drink in the elixir of fly-fishing potential that we provide you, featuring fine printing on top-quality paper. We are terribly excited with our generous, friendly fly-fishing publication and know you will love it also! Please share our joy of discovery and subscribe today!

Strike a deal for only $9.99 for one year.

Order a subscription below for you and your angling friend.

SUBSCRIBE HERE!

Please send me:

☐ One year of **Flyfishing & Tying Journal** for only $9.99 (4 big issues)

☐ Two years of **Flyfishing & Tying Journal** for only $19.95 (8 issues)

☐ Check enclosed (US Funds)   ☐ New   ☐ Renew

☐ Charge to:

☐ Visa ☐ MC CC#:_____ Exp:_____

(Canadian & foreign orders please add $5/year)

Phone orders: 1-800-541-9498 or 503-653-8108. FAX 503-653-2766.
Call 8 to 5 M-F, Pacific Standard Time.

Name:_____

Day Phone:(_____)_____

Address:_____

City:_____ State:_____ Zip:_____

FRANK AMATO PUBLICATIONS • P.O. BOX 82112 • PORTLAND, OR 97282